AF480199

THE ELT HANDBOOK

Dr. Lalit Kumar Yadav

Asst. Professor

Amity Institute of Corporate Communication

Amity University, Noida.

&

Dr. Ruchi Tandon

Asst. Professor

Amity Institute of Corporate Communication

Amity University, Noida.

© Dr.Lalit Kumar Yadav, Dr.Ruchi Tandon

This book has been published with all reasonable efforts taken to make the material error-free after the consent of the author. No part of this book shall be used, reproduced in any manner whatsoever without written permission from the author, except in the case of brief quotations embodied in critical articles and reviews.

Published by

Notion Press Media Pvt. Ltd.

50, Chettiyar Agaram Main Road, Vanagaram, Chennai,

Tamil Nadu 600095

Printed by

Notion Press Media Pvt. Ltd.

50, Chettiyar Agaram Main Road, Vanagaram, Chennai,

Tamil Nadu 600095

ISBN	:	**0000000**
Published on	:	**0000000**
Edition	:	**First**
Price	:	**000.00 INR**

ACKNOWLEDGEMENT

Jai Shri Bala Ji

On the very outset of this book I would like to extend my sincere & heartfelt obligation towards almighty God who helped me in this endeavor.

I also acknowledge with a deep sense of reverence, gratitude towards my parents who have always inspired me by all means.

At last but not least gratitude goes to all of my friends who directly or indirectly helped me to complete this book.

Any omission in this brief acknowledgement does not mean lack of gratitude.

Thanking you

THE ELT HANDBOOK

Table of Contents

Unit 1

APPROACH, METHOD AND TECHNIQUES IN LANGUAGE TEACHING

CONTENTS

1.1 Introduction

1.2 Objectives

1.3 Approach

1.4 Method

1.5 Procedures

1.6 Techniques

1.7 Conclusion

1.8 Summary Point

1.9 Self-Assessment Questions

1.1 Introduction

It is the purpose of this lesson to present three fundamental ideas that are associated with the instruction of the English language at various levels. Approach, method, and technique are the three methods. 'Approach' or theory similar to that of natural approach to teaching language in natural sequence, i.e., hearing, speaking, reading, and writing, is the name given to the fundamental philosophy that is operating behind the processes of teaching language to learners of the English language. The approach is what determines the procedure or methods of instruction, which are collectively referred to as "method."

This can be understood in such a way that if a teacher is of the belief that the natural approach is the best way to teach language to students, then that instructor will choose for the Direct Method methodology. It is inevitable that a variety of approaches to conducting classroom activities or procedures will follow in the wake of the presence of an approach and a method that is pertinent.

The ability to implant a productive combination of language use and usage among the students is made possible by a small number of strategies, such as the conversation practice that is included in the Direct Method classroom. In order to ensure that both teaching and learning are carried out in an efficient manner, this unit will address both theoretical and practical components of language instruction.

1.2 Objectives

By the completion of this lesson, the students will be able to demonstrate the following abilities:

i.   Differentiate between Approach and Method;

ii.   Provide a comprehensive knowledge of the term Technique;

iii.   Make it possible for both the instructor and the student to acquire a comprehension of these words during the entire process of teaching and learning.

1.3 Approaches

In most cases, the term "approaches" is used to refer to collections of concepts, beliefs, and principles that provide the educator with guidance in determining what should be taught, why it should be taught, and how it should be punished. "Where," "what," "why," and "how" are all related to the design and layout of the materials, as well as the classroom approach, which is based on the pre-existing and thus well-considered rationale. "What" refers to the general content, which includes teaching items, topics, themes, and activities.

As a result, an approach is concerned with the theory of the study of language learning and instruction. As a more general term than method, it refers to the investigation of the truths that are obvious to everyone. It is essential to be aware of the fact that a single strategy may incorporate a number of different methodologies. In the context of language learning, an instructional design is typically referred to as an approach when it is relatively explicit at the level of theory of language learning, although it can be applied in many different ways at the level of objectives, teacher and learner roles and activities.

Generally speaking, communicative language instruction is considered to be a method due to the fact that the concepts that underpin it can be utilized in a variety of distinct instances. Teachers who choose to adopt a certain approach have a great deal of leeway in terms of how they might apply the concepts to their unique learning environments.

A set of correlative assumptions that deal with the nature of language instruction and learning in relation to the subject matter that is to be taught is referred to as an approach. Therefore, "Approach" refers to the manner in which a teacher intends to approach the process of information acquisition for his or her students. It is a general guideline that suggests different ways of carrying out a work.

However, it does not list all of the stages that are involved. Rather than that, it doesn't even bother to consider the path to take or the methods of addressing some significant or significant jobs. Therefore, with regard to the significance of approach, it is beneficial to the educator in that it assists in the selection of not only techniques to implement the teaching doctrines, but also in the selection of beneficial experiences for the students in an atmosphere that is favourable to learning through the careful selection of learning materials, resources, and evaluation.

When it comes to the area of English language instruction, often known as ELT, there are two primary techniques that are typically examined by teachers and linguists. These approaches are known as the Behaviourist approach and the Mentalist or Cognitive approach. The behaviourist approach proposes that the learner can acquire knowledge either through the process of habitual formation, which involves stimulus, response, and reinforcement, or through the process of trial and error, which involves rectification.

The mentalist approach, on the other hand, asserts that the learner acquires knowledge through the interaction with their surroundings and the natural influence of a language acquisition brain device (LAD) that is innate to them. By using it, a learner is able to construct and reformulate his own hypothesis, as well as learn the language in a steady and gradual manner.

1.4 Method

One definition of a technique in the field of language instruction is "a practical implementation of an approach." The term "approach" refers to a broad and general theoretical perspective that addresses the "what" and "why" of teaching, as was mentioned earlier. On the other hand, a technique is a particular, practical, and procedural approach that describes the selection and execution of tasks in a classroom setting. In other words, it is concerned with the manner in which or the practical approach to teaching.

Consequently, this is the point at which the theoretical part of teaching, which is an approach, transforms into a practical style of procedure in which decisions are made regarding the information regarding the actual abilities that are going to be taught, as well as the sequence in which the topics are going to be presented. When an instructional design incorporates a particular level of teaching application in terms of objectives, roles for both teachers and students, and activities that take place in the classroom, this phenomenon take place.

In light of this, a technique is defined as the incorporation of predetermined goals, responsibilities for both the instructor and the students, and instructions for engaging in activities. The Grammar Translation, Audio-lingualism, Total Physical Response, and Silent Methods are some examples of things that fall under this category.

However, if we take a look at the grammar-translation technique, we can see that it involves the student learning a number of different grammar rules and then translating the information from the second language into the student's original language. Through a process of deductive learning, students were able to gain the intellectual capacity to comprehend the new language. This was accomplished by learning the rules of the language.

In order to demonstrate how this method was created from the idea that the mind needs to be educated via intellectual exercises in order to be able to do something, the objective of this article is not to criticize this method.

In light of the fact that the behaviourist and mentalist approaches were discussed in section 1.3, it is not surprising that there are audio-lingual and communicative techniques of instruction.

1.5 Procedure

Procedures are the sequence of steps that are taken in order to carry out a process. Techniques are used to describe these step-by-step procedures, which will be covered in the following section. In the context of the grammar-translation approach, the following are examples of conventional procedures:

A piece of writing composed in the second language is read aloud to the class.

1. The first step is for the student to translate the passage from the second language into their native language.

2. The student translates new words from the second language into their own language before discussing them.

3. A grammar rule is presented to the student, and based on the example, the student applies the rule by making use of the introduced vocabulary.

4. The student begins to commit the lexicon of the second language to memory.

A student commits the rules of grammar to memory. By supplying the correct answers, the student is able to rectify any mistakes that they have committed.

When utilizing the grammar-translation approach, this is the process that is utilized, but sometimes with some modifications.

1.6 Techniques

Specifically, a technique is a single practical activity that is based on a procedure that is adopted by the instructor in accordance with the requirements of his or her students. Techniques can be any of the steps that are included in the procedure list that was presented earlier. Different approaches, of course, call for different approaches to be taken.

An example of this would be the Constructivist Approach, which employs the Activity Method, which includes strategies such as role playing and dramatization. Each and every one of these facets of instruction have to be in agreement with each other with the intention of establishing a sense of uniformity. Drills, spoken or written exercises, and exercises that require the completion of sentences are some other examples of approaches.

1.7 Conclusion

The instruction of a language requires a theoretical foundation in the form of approaches, which ultimately result in the execution of procedures in practice. After that, methods are divided down into procedures, and procedures are a collection of approaches for completing a task.

By gaining an understanding of the interrelationships between these notions, a teacher can have a better understanding of the reasoning underpinning their decisions regarding how they choose to teach efficiently, whether through the establishment of habits (the behaviourist approach) or hypotheses (the mentalist approach).

Nevertheless, a teacher cannot be restricted to using any particular method based on any one of the approaches; rather, it is the teacher's own choice to select the method that is the most suitable or multiple methods (eclectic approach), according to the needs of the learners, in order to produce efficient language output among the learners.

1.8 Summary Point

The following are the main points of the unit:

- With regard to the teaching of the English language, there are three notions that are interconnected: approach, method, and technique.

- One definition of an approach is a collection of theoretical concepts concerning the nature of language learning and acquisition.

- Techniques are a collection of activities that are selected by teachers for the goal of achieving maximal proficient output among language learners.

- Methods are the practical execution of theories in the form of procedural ways. Techniques are a group of activities that are based on approaches and methods.

1.9 Self-Assessment Questions

Now after going through the unit, dear students attempt these questions to assess yourlearning rate and pace.

Q.1 Define and elaborate the terms: approach, method and technique. Provide examplesalso in your answer.

Q.2 What are the main approaches and methods based on them in English language teaching? Discuss in detail.

Q.3 Are our language teachers aware of the concepts of approach, method and technique; if so or not what the impact on their teaching language in India is. Give illustrative arguments to prove your point of view.

Unit 2

ROLE OF A TEACHER

CONTENTS

2.1 Introduction

2.2 Objectives

2.3 Teacher's Roles

2.4 Teacher's Evolving Role

2.5 Conclusion

2.6 Summary Points

2.7 Self-Assessment Questions

2.1 Introduction

The requirements of a classroom in the 21st century are obviously significantly different from those of a classroom in the 20th century. In a classroom setting in the 21st century, teachers play the role of facilitators for the learning of their students and producers of productive classroom environments. These environments allow students to develop abilities that they may require in the future or in the present.

However, before we begin to comprehend the ever-evolving function of an English as a second language (ESL) instructor, let us first provide an overview of some of the most in-demand teaching positions that are presently in existence. In his article, Harmer, J. asserts that "it makes more sense to describe different teacher roles and say what they are useful for, rather than making value judgments about the effectiveness of these roles." Let's take a look at some of the most typical responsibilities that teachers play.

2.2 Objectives

By the end of this unit the students will be enabled:

1) To be aware of what a proficient teacher is;

2) To exhibit an in-depth comprehension of the terminology that pertain to the roles of a proficient teacher;

3) To imbue both the teachers and the learners with the knowledge and abilities necessary for teaching and learning procedures.

2.3 Teacher's Roles

Most teachers take on a variety of roles within the classroom. Dear students! Which role do you think most defines your teaching role in the ESL classroom?

The Controller

The teacher is in complete charge of the class, what students do, what they say and how they say it. The teacher assumes this role when a new language is being introduced and accurate reproduction and drilling techniques are needed.

In this classroom, the teacher is mostly the centre of focus, the teacher may have the gift of instruction, and can inspire through their own knowledge and expertise, but does this role really allow for enough student talk time? Is it really enjoyable for the learners? There is also a perception that this role could have a lack of variety in its activities.

The Prompter

The teacher encourages students to participate and makes suggestions about how students may proceed in an activity. The teacher should be helping students only when necessary.

When learners are literally 'lost for words', the prompter can encourage by discreetly nudging students. Students can sometimes lose the thread or become unsure how to proceed; the prompter in this regard can prompt but always in a supportive way.

The Resource

The teacher is a kind of walking resource centre ready to offer help if needed, or provide learners with whatever language they lack when performing communicative activities. The teacher must make her/himself available so that learners can consult her/him when (and only when) it is absolutely necessary.

As a resource the teacher can guide learners to use available resources such as the internet, for themselves, it certainly is not necessary to spoon-feed learners, as this might have the downside of making learners reliant on the teacher.

The Assessor

The teacher assumes this role to see how well students are performing or how well they performed. Feedback and correction are organized and carried out. There are a variety of ways we can grade learners, the role of an assessor gives teachers an opportunity to correctlearners. However, if it is not communicated with sensitivity and support, it could prove counter-productive to a student's self-esteem and confidence in learning the target language.

The Participant

This role improves the atmosphere in the class when the teacher takes part in an activity. However, the teacher takes a risk of dominating the activity when performing it. Here the teacher can enliven a class; if a teacher is able to stand back and not become the centre ofattention, it can be a great way to interact with learners without being too overpowering, hence making it more student-centred classroom.

The Tutor

The teacher acts as a coach when students are involved in project work or self-study. The teacher provides advice and guidance and helps students clarify ideas and limit tasks.

This role can be a great way to pay individual attention to a student. It can also allow a teacher to make tailor a course in order to fit specific student needs. However, it can also lead to a student becoming too dependent or even too comfortable with one teacher and one method or style of teaching.

Now that we've had a chance to look at some of the variety of roles, let us see how we can adopt these into a real classroom activity/task:

ACTIVITY/TASK	HOW THE TEACHER SHOULD BEHAVE
Team game	Energetic, clear, fair, encouraging
Role Play	Supportive, retiring, clear, encouraging
Teacher reading aloud	Dramatic, interesting commanding
Whole class listing	Efficient, clear, supportive

What we notice here is that the roles are often interchangeable. The teacher's role is never static. During the activity we could see an experienced teacher having smooth transition from one role to another.

2.4 Teacher's Evolving Role

Consequently, it is asserted that the classroom of the 21st century is constructed on the assumption that students need to acquire the necessary skills and experiences in order to enter the workplace of the 21st century and to live in a global world. Therefore, the characteristics of the classroom in the 21st century differentiate it from the classroom in the 20th century in that it is more focused on the teaching and learning of the students. Because of this new trend, there is now a greater emphasis placed on the changing roles that teachers play.

Consequently, whilst in the past it was common practice to deliver lectures on a single topic at a time, in the present time, the students' learning is centred around the concept of collaboration. In this particular classroom, for example, the collaborative project-based approach guarantees that the curriculum will grow in the following ways:

- Capacity for higher than average thinking,
- Capacity for effective communication, as well as Students will need to have knowledge of technology in order to be prepared for employment in the 21st century and the more international environment.

The growing English as a Second Language (ESL) instructor must accept new teaching tactics and interactive roles that are drastically different from those that were previously employed. This is despite the fact that there is certainly a place for learning that is centred on the teacher and takes the form of lectures. In addition to this, the curriculum has to be updated so that it is more pertinent to the materials that students would encounter in the 21st century.

Interactive Teacher
A teacher who is fully aware of the dynamics of the group in a

classroom is, by definition, considered to be an interactive teacher. It was explained by Dornyei and Murphey (2003) that the success of classroom learning is highly dependent on the following factors:

- The manner in which students interact with one another and with their instructor;

- The nature of the classroom setting;

- The extent to which students are able to efficiently collaborate and communicate with one another;

- The roles that are not only played by the instructor but also by the students themselves.

According to Brown, H. Douglas (2007), "teachers can play many roles in the course of teaching, and this might not only facilitate learning but also help students learn." The degree to which they are able to successfully carry out these tasks will, of course, be directly proportional to the level of knowledge and expertise that they possess, as well as the interpersonal connection that they cultivate with their students.

According to Harmer, J. (2007), the term "facilitator" is used by a number of authors to describe a specific type of educator. This type of educator is democratic, meaning that the teacher shares some of the leadership with the students, as opposed to autocratic, meaning that the teacher is in control of everything that occurs in the classroom. Additionally, this type of educator encourages learners' autonomy, meaning that students not only learn on their own but also take responsibility for their own learning, by utilizing group and pair work and by acting more as a resource than a transmitter of knowledge.

2.5 Conclusion

Learning is empowering for both the student and the instructor, and it frees the teacher from many of the constraints that being a "expert" could entail. Facilitating learning is a rewarding experience for both parties. If a teacher were to say anything like, "I don't know, let us find out," or "I don't know, do any of you students know the answer?" in the past, it would have been seen a sign of weakness. However, the times have changed, and the function of the English Language Teacher (ELS) must also adapt.

I am hope that the next time you are in charge of instructing a class, you would give some thought to how your role might influence the learning of your pupils. Do your lessons revolve around the teacher, with you managing everything and constantly being in the centre of the action? On the other hand, are you able to "let it go" and give pupils the opportunity to take the spotlight?

Regardless of the tasks that they take on, teachers are responsible for shaping the atmosphere of their classrooms, enhancing the learning of their students, and having an impact on both practice and production. It is a common misconception that a teacher's influence and authority are diminished as they transition from the role of an expert to that of a facilitator. However, this is not the case at all.

2.6 Summary

The following is a list of the primary points that summarize the unit:

- The changing requirements of the classroom in the 21st century necessitate teachers to adjust their duties correspondingly.

- The classrooms of the 21st century are student-centered in order to provide students with the tools necessary to meet the changing expectations of the world.

- There are a variety of roles that teachers are required to play, and these roles vary according to the goals and purposes of their teaching.

- As a result, a teacher can perform the functions of a controller, a resource coordinator, an assessor, an organizer, and a tutor to their students.

- There are no limitations placed on teachers, and they are not limited to taking on only one function at a time.

- They have the ability to take on a variety of roles for a single activity at a given moment in time.

- One of the most important things to keep in mind is that the instructor needs to cultivate an engaging relationship with the students, which will ultimately result in interactive classrooms.

2.7 Self-Assessment Questions

Q.1 What do you think about the demands from the teachers in currently changing classroom environments; illustrate your answer with any current India example.

Q.2   Elaborate various roles of a teacher with reference to the India classrooms; explain further how a teacher can have transition from one role to the other according to the objectives of the learning activities.

Q.3   Describe your own teaching role, which usually you take up in your classes. Also mention, which role you want to adopt in future after reading this unit. Please do not forget to state the level and activities for your class.

Unit 3

THE GRAMMAR TRANSLATION METHOD

CONTENTS

3.1 Introduction

3.2 Objectives

3.3 Characteristics

3.4 Why Grammar Translation Method?

3.5 Procedure of Grammar Translation Method

3.6 Strengths

3.7 Weaknesses

3.8 Conclusion

3.9 Summary Points

3.10 Self-Assessment Questions

3.1 Introduction

It is quite important to have a good teaching approach in order to be successful in accomplishing the goals of teaching within the context of the teaching-learning process. However, procedures alone are not sufficient to assure success unless they are managed by teachers who are both knowledgeable and effective. Many approaches have been utilized in our nation for the purpose of teaching English; nevertheless, the majority of these approaches have been conventional, and any new developments in the field have been ignored.

An appropriate illustration of this would be the application of the Grammar Translation Method. Due to the fact that this approach has numerous reasons for being famous throughout all of time, this unit is specifically designed to examine the method itself in a quick manner as well as its present use in our country. A way of teaching foreign languages that is drawn from the traditional approach of teaching Greek and Latin is known as the Grammar Translation way.

During sessions that focus on grammar translation, students first acquire knowledge of grammatical rules and then put those principles into practice by translating sentences between the target language and their initial language. In other cases, students who are more advanced may be needed to translate entire passages word for word. There are two primary objectives of the method:

- To facilitate the reading and translation of literature published in the target language by students.

- The second is to enhance the students' overall intellectual growth. For the purpose of gaining a comprehensive comprehension of this strategy, let us now examine it in great detail in the following sections

3.2 Objectives

By the end of this unit the students will be enabled to:

i. Understand Grammar Translation Method;

ii. Give an elaborate understanding of the techniques involved in this method;

iii. Understand the terms; the teacher and learner in the

teaching –learning procedure.

3.3 Characteristics

In spite of the fact that there are a lot of innovative approaches and strategies, the Grammar Translation Method (GTM) has been and continues to be one of the most popular approaches to teaching English in our country. The reason for this is due to the following characteristics:

- The majority of the time, classes are communicated in the native tongue.

- A significant amount of vocabulary is presented in the form of lists of individual words.

- Pronunciation receives little to no attention, which makes it simple for teachers to understand all that is being said.

- It is recommended that reading challenging materials be started at an early age.

- Learning a foreign language or a target language is based on the premise that one should be able to read literature written in that language.

- As a result, the primary emphasis of GTM is placed on reading and writing.

- Explanations of the complexities of grammar are provided in the form of grammar rules in the mother tongue, which are then followed by the translation of sentences and texts into and out of the target language. These explanations are lengthy and detailed. According to Stern (1983), "The first language is maintained as the reference system in the acquisition of the target language" (page 455) throughout other words, Stern is absolutely correct in his assertion.

- This approach is used to teach language to the vast majority of language teachers, who themselves were taught language.

3.4 Why Grammar Translation Method?

The question that emerges now is, why would I choose to utilize this method? Yes, the answer is:

One of the primary objectives of GTM is the application of grammar and the correct structuring of sentences. When it comes to teaching kids how to write and read correctly in another language, this is especially helpful since it gives them the opportunity to study interchangeable words and phrases (that is, different terms for different tenses) in a more efficient manner than a verbal teaching method would. It is not difficult to develop tests that test various translations and grammar rules.

Due to the fact that students are directly translating material into another language, it is not necessary for them to participate in classroom activities or learning games. Teachers who are not fluent in English but are fluent in the other language that the pupils typically use are able to teach English using this method with ease. This is because the focus is not placed on the spoken word but rather on translations. Those who support this translation are of the opinion that it may be interpreted most effectively by a student through the use of words, phrases, and sentences. The structure of English is difficult to understand, but it can be simplified by comparing and contrasting it with the structure of the learners' mother tongue. Additionally, the students are able to attempt easy composition activities with the assistance of this strategy.

3.5 Procedure of Grammar Translation Method

Reading material serves as a source at the beginning of the process associated with teaching English or target grammar. It is utilized by the instructor in order to translate words, phrases, and sentences into the native language of the student studying it. For the purpose of being copied, teachers write the same thing on the blackboard recorded in the students' notebooks after being committed to memory.

The understanding of grammatical rules, such as those pertaining to conjunctions and parts of speech, is the primary focus of the majority of the lessons. All of this is being done with the intention of assisting in the internalization of the English structural patterns.

3.6 Strength

Following are the strengths of the Grammar Translation Method (GTM):

- It proceeds from known (mother tongue) to unknown (target or second language).

- Students learn a lot of vocabulary.

- Reading and writing skills are excelled.

- It activates students´ memory.

- It is a time saving easy method for both of the teachers and the taught for the purpose of teaching and learning English grammar.

- The students' grasp of English grammar can be assessed easily and quickly.

- It gives the chance of learning a new language using textbooks.

- Students can learn vocabulary not only in the target language but also in theirmother tongue.

3.7 Weakness

Following are the shortcomings of the Grammar Translation Method (GTM):

- It ignores the natural sequence of learning a language, which is listening, speaking,reading and writing.

- It cannot cater the need to improve listening and speaking.

- Thus students have then unnatural and inaccurate Pronunciation.

- GTM is not interactive and engaging for students.

- It binds the language with the rules of Grammar

3.8 Conclusion

Despite the fact that GTM is subject to criticism for not strengthening students' capacity to use language in real-life situations, it does have several advantages that are intrinsic to it. In order to achieve more productive language output, it is up to the teachers to figure out how to handle it. It is comparable to a backbone in the process of teaching and learning the English language, particularly in our country, because the acquisition of grammar is essential for the correct or accurate communication of both written and spoken words.

Consequently, we are unable to completely give it up; rather, we are required to make use of it in a thoughtful and prudent manner in order to cultivate the students' levels of competence (knowledge) and to improve their overall performance.

3.9 Summary

- An overview of the unit's main points is presented here. The Grammar Translation method (GTM) is the most consistently reliable approach that is utilized in the process of teaching and learning English in our nation.

- It possesses a multitude of qualities, such as the integration of translation and grammar, which enables learners to read literature in the target language, the study and teaching of grammatical principles prior to translation from and to the mother tongue, and the emphasis placed on reading and writing in addition to correctness.

- GTM offers a number of benefits, including the fact that it is a simple and time-saving procedure.

- Grammar can be taught and learned by making use of the pupils' native language, which is a possibility.

- The evaluation of the level of comprehension is a relatively simple task for educators.

- GTM has a number of shortcomings, including the fact that it is an unnatural method, that it does not take into account communication skills such as speaking and listening, and that it places a focus on grammatical rules (competence) while ignoring language usage (performance or skills).

3.10 Self-Assessment Questions

Q.1 Grammar Translation Method is a prevalent method of teaching and learning English language in India; discuss with examples.

Q.2 Do you think main characteristics of GTM make it still a valuable method in current requirements of English language teaching and learning in India?

Q.3 Give a detailed explanation of GTM as a simple combination of the activities of grammar and translation. Support your answer with practical examples of it.

Unit -4

THE COMMUNICATIVE APPROACH

CONTENTS

4.1 Introduction

4.2 Objectives

4.1 Introduction

The fundamental goal of teaching and learning languages is communication, which is covered in this unit. The GTM approach, which we covered in unit four, and all other approaches place a strong emphasis on learning language structures, such as vocabulary and grammatical structures. On the other hand, a communicative approach to teaching places equal emphasis on vocabulary and structure acquisition as well as communication. The primary goal is to provide students and learners with the ability to perform in the language and the knowledge of language usage standards (competence).

In order to carry out linguistic activities like ordering, persuading, agreeing, and promising, we employ language to communicate. Furthermore, as communication is a process, individuals must apply the forms and meanings they have learned to functions in order to negotiate meanings. Oral or written communication between a writer and a reader, or between a speaker and a listener, is crucial in this context. This unit will go into more detail about the communicative teaching strategy and methodology in the sections that follow.

4.2 Objectives

By the end of this unit the students will be enabled to:

    i.   understand the communicative approach

    ii.   give an elaborate understanding of the techniques regarding this method; and

    iii.   get the understanding of these terms in the teaching – learning procedure

4.3 What is Communicative Approach?

The Communicative Approach, often known as Communicative Language Teaching (CLT), is a method of instruction that emphasizes how crucial authentic conversation is to learning. Real conversation and interaction are not only the goal of language learning and teaching, but also the method by which it is accomplished according to the Communicative Approach. This method was first presented in the 1970s and gained popularity as a substitute for the then-dominant systems-oriented approaches and techniques, such the Audio-lingual method.

This indicates that the Communicative Approach aims to improve the learner's competence to communicate in the target language (communicative competence), with an enhanced focus on real-life situations, rather than the acquisition of grammar and vocabulary (grammatical/linguistic competence). Wilkins claims that the communicative approach has moved the emphasis from what language "is" to what language "does." Thus, it entails:

- ❖ a communicative purpose,

- ❖ a desire to communicate,

- ❖ mostly content and not the form (structure),

- ❖ variety of language, and

- ❖ motivation

This change has had a huge impact on classroom materials, course books, teaching techniques and the teacher's role in the classroom, and still influences English language teaching and learning up to this day.

4.4 Some Key Features of Communicating Approach

Lessons contain communicative goals, which is one of the Communicative Approach's primary characteristics. The primary objective of CLT is meaning communication, and language is viewed as a tool to help learners accomplish this goal. As a result, rather than emphasizing grammatical ability, the syllabus for courses that use a Communicative Approach to teaching favours lesson objectives that will help students practice and build their linguistic competence. Various syllabi were developed to accomplish this goal, one of which is the functional-notional syllabus, which allows students to concentrate on the meaning (function) of language and practice it in an authentic environment.

In addition, since developing the four skills—Reading, Writing, Speaking, and Listening—is essential for pupils to achieve real-world objectives, the syllabus may also include work on these areas. The so-called integrated-skills strategy frequently involves working with the skills concurrently. For example, during a listening session, students might be asked to view an online video and leave a remark expressing their thoughts about it. Rather than merely inviting students to provide feedback, educators should specifically address the language, vocabulary, and register relevant to this text, including the writing ability into a listening lesson.

When using the Communicative Approach, this is preferred since it appears more realistic—in real communication, skills are rarely used alone, and an integrated skills approach mimics real-world scenarios. Another crucial factor is the source of the texts used in skills courses. Authentic texts are typically preferred in the Communicative Approach because they may expose students to a more real-world application of language.

By using this teaching strategy, the instructor facilitates the students' learning. The Communicative Approach places the student at the centre of the learning process. This indicates that compared to earlier approaches like audio-lingualism and the direct method, the teacher's role has evolved. As a facilitator of the learning process, the teacher's primary duty is to help pupils improve their accuracy and fluency through communicative practice.

Offer a variety of practice exercises to aid students in developing their communicative competence. While authentic communication is the ultimate goal, there is opportunity for exercises and activities that guarantee pupils practice language in a more regulated way while also emphasizing the development of correctness. But these shouldn't be your only options for language practice. Fluency-building activities are an essential component of a Communicative Approach lesson because they allow students to express meanings.

4.5 Activity Types and Classroom Tips

Activities in the Communicative Approach typically encourage student-student interaction and enhance learners' opportunities to communicate because the teacher is no longer the centre of instruction. The exercises listed below can be used to offer students practice using the language; the amount of assistance provided will depend on the lesson's goal, stage, and students' proficiency. However, it is crucial to emphasize that getting students ready for tasks is a crucial first step in finishing them successfully and helping them become more proficient communicators. The following exercises can be included in a class using the Communicative Approach.

Role-plays

In role-plays, learners are given an imaginary situation and are asked to perform a different role or act as themselves in a particular scenario. Role-plays enable learners to imagine themselves in realistic situations and 'rehearse' before they need to use English in real life. They are also fun and motivating for some learners.

Information gap activities

Through information-gap activities, students must communicate with one another to identify the details they are missing in order to complete a task. Missing data could consist of text, figures, or even illustrations. The primary goal is to encourage students to collaborate and communicate in order to share all the knowledge they require.

Jigsaw Activities

Jigsaw activities involve learners reading, listening or performing different tasks at the same time and later sharing what they have done with their peers. For example, half of the students can be asked to watch a video on a certain topic and the other half can be asked to watch a different video, with a different viewpoint. After learners watch the videos and complete tasks for comprehension, they are asked to share what they had found out with their peers.

Open-ended Discussions and Debates

Debates and discussions can be a useful tool for fluency

practice. They enable learners to share their own views on topics and use their communicative resource to convey ideas, make points, and agree and disagree with others. Debates are usually engaging and provide a rich resource for teachers to assess their learners' communicative competence. However, preparation for debates should be done thoroughly to help students succeed.

4.6 Developments of the Communicative Approach

After its advent in the 1970s, the Communicative Approach branched out into different approaches and methodologies that aim at helping learners develop their communicative competence and is now a term that encompasses different approaches to teaching and learning. Some of these approaches are:

- Project-based learning,

- Task-based learning, and

- Content-based instruction

4.7 The Doctrines of the Communicative Approach

Following are the principles of the Communicative Approach:

- Authentic language is used in a real context.

- Communicative competence should be developed which means that the students should be enabled to understand and interpret the speaker's and writer's intentions.

- The target language is the language of the communication and not just mere thesubject of the study.

- Linguistic functions and forms are presented together.

- Students should learn the language at discourse level and

must be aware of cohesion and coherence, binding properties of a language.

- Students should be active in communicative classes in order to express their ideasand opinions.

- Errors are considered a mark of learning.

- Students' success is measured by their fluency and accuracy simultaneously.

- Communicative interaction promotes cooperative relations among students which helps them to work on negotiating meanings within social and situational contexts.

- The teacher's role is that of advisor.

4.8 Conclusion

As a conclusion, we can state that the communicative approach to education takes into account the true goal of language acquisition and instruction, which is communication in authentic settings. Hence, a teacher employing this strategy might use a variety of English teaching techniques based on the needs and goals of the students, the class size, the accessibility of audio-visual aids, the students' ages and abilities, and more. It calls on instructors to be adaptable and use the right strategies for the job at hand.

4.9 Summary

The enumerated points of the unit are as follows:

- The ground breaking Communicative Approach, often known as Communicative Language Teaching (CLT), centers its attention on the primary goal of teaching and learning language: communication.

- It centralizes written and spoken communications' contextualized meanings.

- The mother tongue may be used occasionally, but the target language is used the most of the time.

- Language function and meanings are just as important as form and structure, and they develop at the same time.

- Students are the centre of the classroom, and teachers play the role of facilitators.

- A range of student-centred activities, such as debates and open-ended discussions, could be included, including role-plays, gap-filling exercises, and jigsaw puzzles.

4.10 Self – Assessment Questions

Q.1 Elaborate what you have understood the Communicative Approach and itscharacteristics?

Q.2 Is India utilizing the Communicative Approach to English language instruction as intended?

Q.3 Describe and illustrate the tenets that form the foundation of the Communicative Approach?

Unit 5

THE DIRECT METHOD

CONTENTS

5.6 Strength

5.7 Weaknesses

5.8 Summary

5.9 Conclusion

5.10 Self – Assessment Questions

5.1 Introduction

The Direct Method (DM) was first created in the early 20th century as a response to GTM. When teaching foreign languages, the direct method—also referred to as the natural method—refrains from using the learners' native tongue and instead focuses solely on the target language. It was developed around 1900 in Germany and France, and it differs from the Grammar Translation Method and other conventional techniques.

The Direct Method's central tenet was that learning a second language ought to resemble learning a first language, with a focus on oral communication, natural language usage, avoidance of translation between the two languages, and little to no grammatical rule analysis. Thus, through concept creation, new linguistic forms and functions are absorbed in this technique. Thus, the purpose of this unit is to introduce it as it was and is primarily utilized by teachers to help students build their linguistic performance, or their capacity to act or speak correctly and effectively in everyday situations.

5.2 Objectives

By the end of this unit the students will be enabled to:

i. understand the Direct Method;

ii. give an elaborate understanding of the Techniques involved in direct method;

iii. understand the terms such as the teacher and learner in the teaching – learning procedure.

5.3 Characteristics

Following are the characteristics of DM:

- Classroom instruction is conducted in the target language.

- Grammar is taught inductively.

- Correct pronunciation along with grammar is emphasized.

- Both of the speaking and listening comprehensions or oral skills are taught.

- Only everyday vocabulary and sentences are taught by means of association withdirect objects, actions or in natural contexts.

5.4 Why Should I Use this Method?

In contrast with the GTM, the Direct Method is mostly taken as effective remedy in teaching and learning English language. It can be very effective at creating fluent speakers of the target language who can actually use it to get by in day-to-day situations.

Teachers may also ask the students questions, have them fill in the blanks in an example sentence, or have them read from a work of literature. All of these techniques emphasize the Direct Method's core strength – teaching students to be able to speak the target language rather than merely be able to translate it.

5.5 The Direct Method's (DM) guiding principles

The doctrines that form the foundation of WM are as follows:

- The first step in teaching a language should be teaching reading and writing in the target language. It will, nevertheless, be developed in tandem with speaking ability.

- Students should be assisted in understanding the meanings through the use of classroom objects such as photographs.

- Avoid using one's mother tongue when speaking.

- Rather than acting as an authoritative interpreter, the instructor should take on the role of demonstration.

- Acquiring vocabulary is more natural than learning word lists in an artificial manner.

- Pronunciation needs to be practiced from the start.

- Language acquisition is accelerated and initiated by self-correction.

5.6 Strengths

Following are the advantages of the DM:

- This method is natural one and is focused on question-answer patterns.

- Grammar is taught inductively. So more opportunities are there to listen to spokenlanguage.

- The most important aspect is spoken language, so that pronunciation and grammarare taken into account.

- It strengthens the ability of self-expression in the target language while becoming habitual of thinking even in the target language.

- There is an ample use of AV aids, which makes the language instruction easy,interesting and more concrete.

- Instructions are given in the target language.

- So it is an experience of living in language.

On the one hand, it will be a good chance for students to improve our knowledge about Grammar and to excel our pronunciation, and at the other hand it is a good method for intermediate and advanced teachers to make student´s skills float. Comparing this method with the Grammar Translation, this one will open more doors now

5.7 Weaknesses

Following are the shortcomings or disadvantages of the DM:

- It is inconvenient for large courses; certain subjects, like reading and writing, receive no specific attention.

- The Straightforward Approach might not be as effective for those who are used to teaching or learning through the Grammar Translation Method.

- In addition to stressing student participation in language acquisition, this approach is likely to be time-consuming.

- Students will need to invest more time and energy into engaging in these activities by immersing themselves in a language immersion.

Henry Sweet, the British applied linguist, also pointed out its limitations by asserting that the Direct Method offered innovations at the level of teaching procedures but lacked a thorough methodological basis. Stern has observed (1983) that the Direct Method has embodied the 'first attempt to make the language learning situation one of language use and to train the learner to abandon the first language as the frame of reference' (459).

5.8 Conclusion

In summary, it is abundantly evident that the DM, despite all of the drawbacks mentioned in section 6.7, is incredibly well-liked and well-respected both domestically and internationally. It is a rationalist approach that works well for immediately introducing and instructing students in the target language. It begins with oral practice, drill, and graded frameworks, giving the students a solid foundation in language. Dear students, in spite of all its benefits, you should never stop searching and investigating for fresh approaches and strategies to use in language instruction in order to get more effective results.

5.9 Summary

The enumerated points of the unit are as follows:

- The direct method, in response to GTM, seeks to educate by using the target language in language instruction.

- The usage of one's mother tongue or native language is restricted and should only occur when absolutely required.

- The method's primary focus is on student-centered learning.

- Grammar is taught using inductive reasoning.

- Teachers act as both demonstrators and facilitators.

- Reading and writing skills are integrated with speaking and listening to help students strengthen their speaking and listening abilities.

- By developing the students' concept in the target language, thinking in the target language is concentrated.

- Although the DM's primary priority is fluency, accuracy is also taken into consideration.

- The majority of classroom activities, such as role-playing, jigsaw puzzles, open-ended conversations, and debates, involve oral communication.

- Common vocabulary is taught.

- The purpose of the syllabus is to foster students' capacity for meaning negotiation rather than to provide structure.

- DM has advantages and disadvantages as well. Nonetheless, it's a helpful technique for developing language proficiency.

5.10 Self – Assessment Questions

1. "The Direct Method can be used in conjunction with other methods because it isnot probably a 'method' at all. It is a principle, and it is one of the main principles of psychology of language that can be directly translated into classroom procedure. It can, and should be applied to almost all the teaching of the foreign language: in teaching of grammar, new words, new constructions, and new patterns" (Gurrey 1970, 26); discuss it with illustrations.

2. Explain the use of Direct Method in India situation of teaching and learning English language. Give practical examples to support your answer.

3. Compare and contrast the merits and demerits of GTM and DM.

Unit 6

The Audio Lingual Method

Content

6.1 Introduction

6.2 Objectives

6.3 Characteristics

6.4 Why should I Use this Method?

6.5 The Principles of the ALM

6.6 Strengths

6.7 Weaknesses

6.8 Conclusion

6.9 Summary Points

6.10 Self-Assessment Questions

6.1 Introduction

When teaching foreign languages, one method commonly employed is the audio-lingual method (ALM), sometimes known as the Army Method or New Key. In contrast to GTM, the ALM shares the same objective of improving communication skills as the Direct Method. It is predicated on the Coleman Report's assertion that reading should take precedence over oral skill instruction because teaching oral skills is impractical. The Army Method was the original name of the ALM. The primary sources of inspiration for the creation of the Audio-lingual Method were the works and lectures of C. Fries and R. Lado, the advancement of Contrastive Linguistics, the new technology of language laboratories, and behaviourist psychology's theories of conditioning.

6.2 Objective

By the end of this unit the students will be enabled to:

i.   understand Audio-lingual method;

ii.   give an elaborate understanding of the techniques involved in this method;

iii. get the understanding of these terms in the teaching – learning procedure.

6.3 Characteristics

There are five assumptions, in light of the American Structural Linguistics, for ALM put forward by Moultan, W. G. (1963, 462-3). These assumptions are basis of ALM characteristics:

1. As opposed to writing, which occurs during mother tongue learning, language is speech. It follows that oral presentations should come before written ones from a pedagogical perspective.

2. B. F. Skinner's theory that views language as "verbal behaviour" provides the basis for the idea that a language is a collection of habits. Thus, his operant conditioning, which is predicated on habit formation, has an impact on ALM. This presumption has been used to language instruction through drill, memory, and mimicking.

3. Focus on teaching the language itself, not just its usage. That is strongly opposed to GTM, which emphasizes language use in context rather than language itself.

4. The fourth argument, which is connected to the third, is that a language is defined by what its native speakers say,

not by what others believe they should say. It indicates that the language is spoken by its native speakers, not as grammarians would have it.

5. The final and most crucial premise treats languages as distinct living things. The idea that students should "start with a clean slate" is emphasized by Bloomfield, L. (1942, 1) since different languages have distinct structures, sound patterns, and meanings. As a result, ALM materials offer drills in these opposing locations.

Now based on the above-mentioned assumptions,

Following are the major characteristics of the ALM:

- Material is presented in a dialogue form.

- Structural patterns are taught using repetitive drills.

- There is little or no grammatical explanation.

- Great importance is put onto pronunciation.

- Very little use of the mother tongue by teachers is permitted.

- Vocabulary is strictly limited in context.

6.4 Why Should I Use This Method?

As the GTM, students can learn by repetition. Students pay attention and carry a sequence of what they are doing, but despite of learning it in class, teachers can make activities to be performed at home so they can practice writing and reading. It sounds really boring the fact that students have to repeat only. Teachers might find the way to make it interesting and look for different and funny activities.

6.5 Principles of the ALM

The principles of ALM are as following:

- Language forms occur naturally in some socio-cultural context.

- Students must learn syntax (sentence structure) and parts of speech to adjust theparts of speech in its slot.

- Correct habits are developed through positive reinforcement.

- This is possible only through students' response to the provided stimuli.

- Each language has specific number of structural patterns and practice of these helps to form habits among students. Subsequently it enables the students to use them.

- The students learning should make them use language automatically without stopping to think on it.

- The teacher's role should be that of an orchestra organizer, conducting, guiding, and controlling the students' behaviour.

- Being the language different, they should be kept separate so the mother tongue should not interfere with the learning of the target language and it is possible only to restrict the usage of the mother tongue in the language classroom.

- The language teacher's role should be like that of a native speaker model to be copied by the students for learning it in the best way.

- Errors should be avoided in order to prevent the bad habit formation. That is why drills are used in ALM for the accurate habit formations.

- Natural order of learning a language must be followed in which speech has greater importance than the other skills.

- Language and culture are part and parcel of each other. So cultural contexts should be provided in language teaching.

6.6 Strengths

Following are the strengths of the ALM:

- Automatic learning without stopping is the main strength of the ALM throughdrilling and repetition.

- It is emphasized in sentence production.

- It forms verbal behavior through habit formation.

- The language laboratory and use of audio visual aids are also its tools.

- Takes advantage of pronunciation skills.

- Most part of the lesson is given in the target language

6.7 Weaknesses

Following are some of its weaknesses:

- Too much repetition makes the drill mechanical and not the meaningful ones.

- Errors are necessarily to be avoided at all costs.

- No meaningful learning is there because of just structural forms being drilled in amechanical way.

- There does not develop any relation between form and meanings.

- Takes advantage of pronunciation skills.

- Most part of the lesson is given in the target language.

6.8 Conclusion

Though ALM has certain weaknesses, yet to be short it can be best utilized for its good impacts with inventiveness and resourcefulness on the part of the teacher. It can be done by him or her by varying the careful presentation of the material and creating interesting situations for the students. For this purpose the teachers should be provided with in-service training. The Audio-lingual, in short, is very useful method in developing accurate target language through habit formations.

We conclude our discussion of this method with the summary of H. H. Stern (1983, 465-66) as following: First of all, it is the one of the earlier theories that recommend the development of language on declared linguistic as well as psychological principles. Secondly, it attempts to make language learning accessible to large groups of ordinary learners. Thirdly, it stresses syntactical progressive development unlike the other methods. Fourthly, it leads to the development of simple techniques, while excluding and intensive practice of specific features of the language. And lastly it separates the language skills into a pedagogical device of auditory and oral practice.

The summary points of the unit are as following:

- Language is a system of linguistic structures and ALM is basically the method to promote their learning along with developing the communication skills through habit formation.

- Language is speech and not just writing.

- A language can be learnt through verbal habit formation by means of repetition, drills, stimuli and responses.

- For the above-mentioned purpose reinforcement plays a vital role.

- The use of drills and pattern practice has great benefits in language teaching andlearning.

- Language skills are taught in natural way of listening, speaking, reading and writing.

- Accuracy and fluency are focused.

- Language and culture go side by side.

- Teaching vocabulary is of secondary importance.

6.10 Self-Assessment Questions

1. "The real goal of instruction was an ability to talk the language and not to talk about it". (In Mohrnann, 1961, 88). Give your arguments in favor or against the statement.

2. Discuss with examples the fundamental principles of the Audio-lingual Method.

3. Give your point of view how the Audio-lingual Method can be transformed into a better method according to the requirements of the India students.

Case Study

Case Study 1

Healthcare Communication:

In a bustling hospital, patient dissatisfaction was on the rise despite the quality of medical care provided. Upon investigation, it was revealed that communication breakdowns between medical staff and patients were rampant. Patients often felt confused about their treatment plans or misunderstood medical jargon used by healthcare providers, leading to frustration and dissatisfaction. To tackle this pervasive issue, hospital administrators decided to implement a comprehensive communication skills training program for all healthcare providers.

The training program covered various aspects of effective communication, including empathetic listening, clear explanation of medical procedures in layman's terms, and active engagement with patients to address their concerns and preferences. Role-playing exercises were incorporated into the training sessions to simulate real-life patient interactions and help healthcare providers practice applying their communication skills in different scenarios.

As a result of the communication skills training initiative, significant improvements were observed in patient satisfaction scores. Patients reported feeling more informed about their medical conditions and treatment plans, leading to a greater sense of trust and confidence in the healthcare providers. Moreover, the frequency of misunderstandings and miscommunications decreased, resulting in smoother and more efficient patient care processes.

In addition to the positive impact on patient satisfaction, the communication skills training program also had tangible benefits for healthcare providers. Nurses and doctors reported feeling more confident and competent in their communication skills, which enhanced their job satisfaction and reduced stress levels. Better communication among healthcare teams also led to improved collaboration and coordination, resulting in more seamless patient care delivery and fewer instances of medical errors.

Overall, the investment in communication skills training proved to be a worthwhile endeavour for the hospital, resulting in happier patients, more engaged healthcare providers, and ultimately, better healthcare outcomes for all.

Case Study 2

Cross-Cultural Communication

In an increasingly globalized business environment, an international corporation faced challenges in managing projects across culturally diverse teams. Despite having talented individuals from various cultural backgrounds, misunderstandings and conflicts often arose due to differences in communication styles, norms, and cultural values. These communication barriers not only hindered effective collaboration but also impeded the company's ability to innovate and compete in the global market.

To address this critical issue, the company embarked on a cross-cultural communication initiative aimed at equipping employees with the knowledge and skills needed to navigate cultural differences effectively. The initiative consisted of a series of workshops, seminars, and cultural awareness training sessions designed to promote cultural sensitivity, empathy, and adaptability among team members.

One of the key components of the cross-cultural communication initiative was the promotion of active listening and open-mindedness when interacting with colleagues from different cultural backgrounds. Employees were encouraged to seek clarification and ask questions to better understand each other's perspectives, rather than making assumptions based on stereotypes or preconceived notions.

Another important aspect of the initiative was the emphasis on developing intercultural communication competence, which involved learning how to adjust communication styles and strategies to accommodate the cultural preferences and expectations of others. Through interactive activities and role-playing exercises, employees had the opportunity to practice applying their cross-cultural communication skills in simulated work scenarios.

As a result of the cross-cultural communication initiative, significant improvements were observed in team dynamics, collaboration, and productivity. Employees reported feeling more comfortable and confident working with colleagues from diverse cultural backgrounds, leading to enhanced teamwork and synergy.

Moreover, the company saw an increase in innovation and creativity as team members brought diverse perspectives and insights to problem-solving and decision-making processes.

In conclusion, the investment in cross-cultural communication proved to be invaluable for the company, enabling it to leverage the full potential of its diverse workforce and gain a competitive edge in the global marketplace. By fostering a culture of inclusivity, respect, and understanding, the company was able to create an environment where cultural differences were celebrated as strengths rather than barriers to success.

Case Study 3

Leadership Communication

In a manufacturing company plagued by low morale and high turnover rates, poor communication from upper management was identified as a significant issue. Employees felt disconnected and undervalued, leading to a decline in engagement and productivity across the organization. Recognizing the critical role that effective leadership communication plays in driving employee engagement and retention, the company decided to invest in a comprehensive leadership communication training program for its managers and supervisors.

The leadership communication training program was designed to equip managers with the skills and strategies needed to communicate effectively with their teams, build trust and rapport, and foster a culture of open communication and transparency within the organization. The program covered various topics, including active listening, providing constructive feedback, conflict resolution, and leading difficult conversations.

One of the key objectives of the training program was to help managers understand the impact of their communication style and behaviour on employee morale and performance. Through self-assessment tools and feedback sessions, managers were able to identify areas for improvement and develop action plans to enhance their communication skills and leadership effectiveness.

Another important aspect of the leadership communication training program was the emphasis on leading by example and modeling the desired behaviours. Managers were encouraged to demonstrate authenticity, empathy, and integrity in their communication with employees, creating a culture of trust and psychological safety where employees felt comfortable voicing their opinions and concerns.

As a result of the leadership communication training initiative, significant improvements were observed in employee engagement, morale, and retention. Employees reported feeling more valued and appreciated by their managers, leading to higher levels of job satisfaction and commitment to the organization. Moreover, the company saw a reduction in turnover rates and absenteeism, resulting in cost savings and increased productivity.

In conclusion, the investment in leadership communication proved to be a wise decision for the manufacturing company, enabling it to create a positive work environment where employees felt heard, respected, and empowered to contribute their best work. By equipping managers with the skills and tools needed to communicate effectively, the company was able to drive employee engagement and retention, ultimately leading to improved business performance and success.

Case Study 4

Crisis Communication

A retail chain found itself in the midst of a public relations crisis following a product recall that affected thousands of customers. The initial response from the company was criticized for being slow, vague, and insufficient, leading to widespread panic, confusion, and outrage among consumers. Recognizing the urgent need to regain control of the narrative and rebuild trust with customers, the company swiftly implemented a crisis communication strategy aimed at addressing the concerns and needs of those affected by the recall.

The first step in the crisis communication strategy was to provide timely and transparent updates to customers, informing them of the details surrounding the product recall, the potential risks involved, and the steps being taken to rectify the situation. This was done through a variety of channels, including press releases, social media posts, and direct communication with affected customers via email or phone.

In addition to providing factual information, the company also made a concerted effort to demonstrate empathy and concern for the well-being of its customers. This involved acknowledging the inconvenience and distress caused by the recall, expressing regret for any harm or inconvenience caused, and outlining the company's commitment to resolving the issue in a timely and responsible manner.

Another key aspect of the crisis communication strategy was to actively engage with customers and address their questions, concerns, and complaints in a prompt and respectful manner. This involved setting up dedicated customer service hotlines, email addresses, and social media channels staffed by trained representatives who were equipped to handle inquiries and provide assistance to affected customers.

As a result of the crisis communication efforts, the company was able to mitigate the damage caused by the product recall and rebuild trust with customers over time. By providing transparent and empathetic communication, the company demonstrated its commitment to putting customer safety and satisfaction first, ultimately preserving its reputation and restoring

Case Study 5

Sales Communication

A technology start-up had developed a ground breaking product with the potential to revolutionize the industry, but despite its innovative features and capabilities, the company struggled to generate significant sales. After conducting a thorough analysis of the sales process, it became evident that one of the primary obstacles was the lack of effective communication skills among the sales team.

Many sales representatives were proficient in product knowledge and technical expertise, but they lacked the ability to effectively communicate the value proposition of the product to potential customers. They struggled to articulate the benefits of the product in a compelling and persuasive manner, resulting in missed opportunities and lost revenue.

To address this critical issue, the company decided to invest in a sales communication training program aimed at equipping sales representatives with the skills and strategies needed to communicate effectively with customers and close more deals. The training program covered various aspects of sales communication, including active listening, questioning techniques, objection handling, and persuasive communication.

One of the key components of the training program was the development of a tailored sales pitch that highlighted the unique features and benefits of the product in a way that resonated with the needs and priorities of the target audience. Sales representatives were trained to identify customer pain points, ask probing questions to uncover underlying needs, and position the product as the ideal solution to address those needs.

In addition to improving their verbal communication skills, sales representatives also received training on non-verbal communication techniques, such as body language and facial expressions, to enhance their ability to build rapport and establish trust with customers. Role-playing exercises and simulated sales scenarios were incorporated into the training sessions to provide hands-on practice and feedback.

As a result of the sales communication training initiative, significant improvements were observed in the performance of the sales team. Sales representatives reported feeling more confident and competent in their ability to communicate effectively with customers, resulting in increased sales conversions and revenue generation for the company. Moreover, the company saw a positive impact on customer satisfaction and loyalty as sales representatives became better equipped to address customer needs and concerns.

In conclusion, investing in sales communication training is essential for companies looking to improve sales performance and drive business growth. By equipping sales representatives with the skills and strategies needed to communicate effectively with customers, companies can increase their competitive advantage and achieve greater success in the marketplace.

Case Study 6

Academic Communication

A prestigious university was experiencing a decline in student engagement and academic performance, prompting concerns among faculty and administrators. After conducting a comprehensive assessment of the factors contributing to the decline, it became apparent that one of the key issues was the lack of effective communication between faculty and students.

Students reported feeling disconnected from their instructors and frustrated by the lack of clarity in course materials and assignments. They struggled to understand expectations and requirements, leading to confusion and anxiety about their academic progress. In response to these concerns, the university decided to implement a series of communication skills workshops for both faculty and students.

The workshops focused on various aspects of academic communication, including effective listening, clear articulation of ideas, and constructive feedback. Faculty members were trained to communicate course objectives and expectations clearly, provide timely feedback on assignments, and engage students in meaningful discussions and interactions. Students, on the other hand, were taught how to actively participate in class discussions, ask questions, and seek clarification when needed.

In addition to the workshops, the university also implemented changes to its course materials and syllabi to make them more accessible and understandable to students. This included using plain language, organizing information in a logical manner, and providing examples and explanations to clarify complex concepts.

As a result of these initiatives, significant improvements were observed in student engagement and academic performance. Students reported feeling more confident and supported in their academic pursuits, leading to increased motivation and enthusiasm for learning. Faculty members also reported greater satisfaction with their teaching experiences, as they felt better equipped to communicate effectively with their students and facilitate meaningful learning experiences.

Overall, the investment in communication skills training and initiatives proved to be beneficial for both students and faculty, creating a more inclusive and supportive learning environment where communication barriers were addressed, and academic success was prioritized.

Case Study 7

Conflict Resolution

A growing technology start-up was experiencing frequent conflicts among team members, which were hindering productivity and morale. Despite the company's innovative products and talented employees, unresolved conflicts were creating tension and discord within the team, impacting collaboration and creativity. In response to these challenges, the company decided to implement a conflict resolution training program aimed at equipping employees with the skills and strategies needed to manage conflicts effectively.

The conflict resolution training program focused on various aspects of conflict management, including active listening, empathy, and negotiation. Employees were taught how to identify the underlying causes of conflicts, communicate assertively and respectfully, and work collaboratively towards mutually acceptable solutions. Role-playing exercises and case studies were used to provide practical examples and opportunities for employees to practice their conflict resolution skills in simulated scenarios.

One of the key objectives of the training program was to promote a culture of open communication and trust within the organization, where employees felt comfortable addressing conflicts constructively and seeking assistance when needed. Managers and team leaders were also trained to serve as mediators and facilitators in conflict resolution processes, providing guidance and support to employees as they worked through their differences.

As a result of the conflict resolution training initiative, significant improvements were observed in team dynamics and collaboration. Employees reported feeling more confident and empowered to address conflicts proactively, leading to a reduction in the frequency and severity of conflicts within the team. Moreover, the company saw an increase in productivity and innovation as employees were able to focus their energy and attention on their work, rather than on interpersonal conflicts.

In conclusion, investing in conflict resolution training is essential for companies looking to foster a positive work environment and maximize team performance. By equipping employees with the skills and strategies needed to manage conflicts effectively, companies can minimize the negative impact of conflicts on productivity and morale, and create a culture of collaboration and innovation.

Case Study 8

Customer Service Communication

A leading hospitality chain was facing challenges with customer satisfaction and retention due to poor communication skills among its customer service representatives. Despite the company's commitment to providing exceptional service, customers often reported feeling frustrated and undervalued when interacting with frontline staff. Recognizing the critical role that effective communication plays in delivering a positive customer experience, the company decided to invest in a comprehensive customer service communication training program for its employees.

The customer service communication training program focused on various aspects of communication, including active listening, empathy, and problem-solving. Employees were taught how to greet customers warmly, listen attentively to their needs and concerns, and communicate clearly and effectively to address any issues or inquiries. Role-playing exercises and simulations were used to provide practical examples and opportunities for employees to practice their communication skills in realistic scenarios.

One of the key objectives of the training program was to empower employees to take ownership of customer interactions and ensure that every customer felt valued and appreciated. Employees were encouraged to go above and beyond to exceed customer expectations and create memorable experiences that would inspire loyalty and repeat business.

As a result of the customer service communication training initiative, significant improvements were observed in customer satisfaction and retention. Customers reported feeling more satisfied and appreciated when interacting with frontline staff, leading to increased loyalty and positive word-of-mouth referrals. Moreover, the company saw a reduction in customer complaints and escalations, as employees became more adept at addressing issues proactively and resolving them to the customer.

Case Study 9

Public Speaking

A non-profit organization was struggling to raise awareness of its cause and attract support from donors due to ineffective public speaking at fundraising events and community outreach programs. Despite having a compelling mission and impactful programs, the organization's speakers often lacked confidence and clarity when presenting to audiences, resulting in missed opportunities to engage and inspire potential supporters. Recognizing the importance of effective public speaking in conveying its message and mobilizing support, the organization decided to invest in a public speaking training program for its staff and volunteers.

The public speaking training program focused on various aspects of public speaking, including vocal delivery, body language, and storytelling. Participants were taught how to project confidence and authority, capture audience attention, and deliver persuasive messages that resonated with listeners. Practical exercises and rehearsals were incorporated into the training sessions to provide opportunities for participants to practice their public speaking skills and receive constructive feedback from trainers and peers.

One of the key objectives of the training program was to empower participants to become effective advocates for the organization's mission and programs. Participants were encouraged to share their personal stories and experiences, connect emotionally with the audience, and inspire action through their words and actions.

As a result of the public speaking training initiative, significant improvements were observed in the organization's ability to engage and mobilize support from donors and stakeholders. Speakers reported feeling more confident and prepared when presenting to audiences, leading to more impactful and memorable presentations. Moreover, the organization saw an increase in donations and support as speakers became more effective at communicating the organization's mission and impact, inspiring others to get involved and make a difference.

In conclusion, investing in public speaking training is essential for non-profit organizations looking to raise awareness of their cause and mobilize support from donors and stakeholders. By equipping staff and volunteers with the skills and confidence needed to communicate effectively and persuasively, organizations can amplify their message and drive positive change in their communities and beyond.

Case Study 10

Virtual Communication

In response to the COVID-19 pandemic, a global corporation transitioned to remote work to ensure the safety and well-being of its employees. While the shift to remote work enabled employees to continue their work remotely, it also presented challenges in maintaining effective communication and collaboration across virtual teams. Many employees struggled to adapt to the virtual work environment and found it difficult to communicate and collaborate effectively with colleagues who were physically distant. Recognizing the importance of effective virtual communication in ensuring business continuity and employee engagement, the company decided to invest in a virtual communication training program for its employees.

The virtual communication training program focused on various aspects of virtual communication, including video conferencing etiquette, email communication best practices, and remote collaboration tools. Participants were taught how to communicate clearly and effectively in virtual meetings, engage and connect with colleagues remotely, and leverage technology to facilitate collaboration and teamwork. Practical exercises and simulations were incorporated into the training sessions to provide opportunities for participants to practice their virtual communication skills and receive feedback from trainers and peers.

One of the key objectives of the training program was to empower participants to overcome the challenges of virtual communication and thrive in the remote work environment. Participants were encouraged to develop strategies for managing distractions, setting boundaries, and fostering a sense of connection and belonging with their virtual colleagues.

As a result of the virtual communication training initiative, significant improvements were observed in employee productivity, engagement, and satisfaction. Employees reported feeling more confident and competent in their ability to communicate effectively in virtual settings, leading to smoother and more efficient collaboration across virtual teams. Moreover, the company saw a reduction in misunderstandings and miscommunications as employees became more adept at leveraging virtual communication tools and techniques to stay connected and aligned.

In conclusion, investing in virtual communication training is essential for companies looking to maximize the benefits of remote work and ensure the success of their virtual teams. By equipping employees with the skills and strategies needed to communicate effectively and collaborate remotely, companies can overcome the challenges of virtual work and achieve their business objectives in the digital age.

www.ingramcontent.com/pod-product-compliance
Lightning Source LLC
Chambersburg PA
CBHW040731120726

48010CB00002B/77